Evanescent memories

by

A.B. Andersson

Cover illustration: Stefan Eriksson (www.stefaneriksson.se)
Translation: Paul Lambert/Copypanthers (www.copypanthers.com)
Publisher and printer: BoD
ISBN: 978-91-7463-473-0

Introduction

In the summer of 2012, poet A.B. Andersson had his book debut with a collection under the original Swedish title of *Flyktingens syn*. This was the first time ever that any of his poems came out in print – more than fifty years after his death. The collection received an unexpectedly large amount of attention, especially in the regions around Barva and Sörmland. In order to celebrate this unexpected success, a new edition of *Flyktingens syn* was published.

The new edition, which has also been released in this English-language rendition, features an added poem, a revised foreword as well as a more elaborate typography.

Foreword

One September afternoon some years ago, my grandmother handed me a stack of handwritten papers. Most of these old yellowed papers contained beautiful poems. My grandmother told me that they were written by her grandfather, August Bernhard Andersson. Solveig, as my grandmother is named (also co-publisher of the collection you hold in your hands), had saved these poems for us, his posterity, to share.

August Bernhard Andersson (1877-1961) was a farmer by profession, and continued in that occupation until the middle of the 1950s, at which time a son of his took over the farm at Barva parish, located near the town of Eskilstuna. However, the farm had been in the same family since the middle of the 17th century.

In actual fact, however, August did not tend to the farm himself. The work in the fields was primarily done by his sons. The enterprise for which A.B. Andersson himself would be most remembered in particular was of a municipal, but also religious, nature. He was also very active within the temperance movement. He took part in a number of associations; among such positions, he was a member of the municipal council, and he served as treasurer for the local division of *Folkpartiet* (the Swedish Liberal Party). He was the chairman of the Sobriety Council, as well as a member of the Barva Blue Ribbon Association (a temperance society). He served many years on the parish council and on the church council, fifty-five years as a board member for the Barva Equine Insurance Association, and twenty-five years as secretary for the Barva Fruit Growers' Association, a position that earned him a silver medal from the Swedish Royal Patriotic Society for his contributions within the field of horticulture. This last distinction is what gave him particular recognition in his part of the country.

> *In the end, Mr. Andersson's writing was among the better of the rich flora of such 'service letters'. The man behind the pen is enthusiastic and always ready for action.*

These beautiful words are an excerpt from an article published by the *Eskilstunakuriren* (newspaper) soon after he was awarded the said medal[1]. Not only do the lines tell us something about the work for which A.B. Andersson was known during his lifetime, but many of his exploits would later re-emerge in the form the of motifs and themes found in his poems.

Solveig described him as a kind, loving man with a good sense of humour – something to which several of his poems bear witness. Many of the pieces that have

---

[1] *Eskilstunakuriren,* 2 Dec. 1943, author not given

been found in more recent times tells us of a man who on one hand was extremely dedicated to his friends and family, but who on the other hand did not balk at describing them with the help of a little bit of humour.

He was often very well dress and was delighted to show off his new suits. Both verse and prose were his great lifelong passions.

August Bernhard Andersson died on Tuesday, 3 January 1961, and was buried at Barva cemetery. He was 84 years old.

August Bernhard Andersson

After his death, the poems remained idle and in Solveig's safekeeping. With the exception of a second handwritten copy being made in the mid-1950s in order to make the poems more legible, the poems have largely been left unread, until recently.

When I received the poems (in the autumn of 2006), they were put into a binder, which in turn ended up on a shelf. There they once more became more or less forgotten. After a few years had passed and after I moved house a few times, I found the binder once more. As I leafed through the yellowed pages, what I saw of what I could read of the archaic longhand, were beautiful poems, sonnets and song lyrics. The language was flowery and colourful. The content was of a deep and musing nature, focussing on people, destiny, diligence, work, clean living, spirituality and faith. Sometimes there was even a message or a few words of wisdom contained within the text. In particular, there were recurring warnings about the dangers that drinking poses.

I spend a few days, along with Solveig, rewriting these texts and processing them into book form. Our common goal has been to publish them in print. This has been a very pleasant collaboration for us both. Yet, I would like to think that this work not only does A.B. Andersson justice, as this is so much more than a mere heirloom; it is a hidden treasure from the previous century that has now been brought back into the light. It is a heritage from a poet who never got the recognition he deserved while he still lived. It is my hope that you will perhaps buy this book (or borrow it from the library for that matter) and that you will read it and enjoy it.

A.B. Andersson got around to writing many poems during his life; this book only contains a small selection of them. Some of the poems have been lost over the years (most of the poems were written at the end of the 19th century, after all!). Other poems have been kept out for personal reasons. None of the content has been changed for publication[2]. Only the slightest changes were made to the typography within the poems themselves, and then only where there were absolutely necessary. Even the author's commentaries and reflections were found among the original papers; we have naturally included them in this collection. We thought that the readers would find these interesting as well.

The book shares its title with one of the poems contained within. I thought it was a very beautiful poem, whose title fit the overall content in the book. If you will bear with me, I would like to take the opportunity to conclude this foreword with a few words about the intention behind the title.

Poetry is an art form that is highly open to interpretation. *Evanescence* can, under these circumstances, be interpreted in several ways. A personal interpretation of the *evanescent* is that of the *fleeting, passing* or *transient*. The flower in the poem *The evanescent memory* becomes a symbol of that very idea,

---

[2] **Editor's note:** Poetry is among the most difficult to translate from a language to another. A literal translation of the content is almost impossible, especially with regard to aesthetic elements, such as verse and rhyme. However, for this English edition, some great work has been done to preserve the content as far as it's been possible.

and what remains for the beholder – who in this case is the protagonist in the poem – is a mere memory and a thought of what he had seen. Something has slipped away from him! These are some of the feelings to which August Bernhard Andersson often returns.

The sense of transience and evanescence is constantly present. They can be seen in the way the sun rises and sets, as well as in life and death, harvest and the seasons, and not least, sin and arrogance giving way to spiritual purity. It is about everything that meets its destiny.

> *But while the lily withers each year*
> *Hope brings it back into bloom*

says August, and thereby captures the spirit of the entire compilation.

J.O. Hasselkvist
Örebro, 27 June 2012 // Borås, 2013

Acknowledgements

Prior to the publication of the compilation, we had been in correspondence with the Barva Historical Society, Ewa Gustafsson from Kafjärdens Congregation, as well as with relatives who still live in the parish to this day. You have all been a tremendous help. Our deepest thanks!

Thanks as well go to Stefan Eriksson, who designed the cover.

A special thanks to Paul for his excellent work with the translation into English, and to Deniz, for supervising the process.

Also, thanks to all of you who commented and gave us your reflections and ideas on the working process; especially concerning the title of the collection. We did choose this title after all, not only because of the beauty of the poem, but since it felt like most accurate concerning the circumstances of the book. For what is this, of not a collection of memories, now saved from the risk of fade into oblivion.

From the publishers

A Poem of Inspiration

I walk into the peaceful night.
On times to come, I ponder.
A dream, once vague, now firmly in sight
Takes lead of whither I wander.

How fair is all that we behold,
Should only we choose to see.
As aught is now as in times of old,
I fear not the tempest to be.

So many woeful sighs I'll hear,
See many mirages of doom.
But while the lily withers each year,
Hope brings it back into bloom.

Toward the sky, its stalk extends
Yielding not but for the gales.
Its angelic fragrance to descend
As time on its course sets sail.

Toward me shall smile a lily fair
With brilliance and with joy.
A beauty beyond all worldly compare,
Free of falsehood and spiteful ploy.

Lest that fate should turn away its face
And cruelly obscure its shimmer,
But reach out and take me to into its embrace,
While the life in my being still glimmers.

A wonderful path that leads us all
Without hinder, full of promise.
Should we but let our designs to fall
Forever shame be upon us.

And once the passionate finally rest
From their varied thoughts written here,
Nought can keep them from taking form
For the one that he holds dear.

The Rights of Man
(A Song of Suffrage)[3]

Heaven saw fit to set man free
'twas decreed in days of old.
As a result, and so it must be,
There are men whose purses hold
More wealth than they could ever spend.
Such excess is hard to defend.
Is this not iniquity?

You wretched men with swollen heads
Your right to rule, you declaim.
You'd think not twice 'fore stealing bread
From the blind man or the lame.
Yet the day approach, when all shall see
Your fall from grace; our enmity
Shall strike against your person.

---

[3] **Author's note:** Many years ago in the *Eskilstuna-Kuriren*, there was a poem entitled *Rättvisan* ["Justice"]. I thought that I should try to write a poem in the same vain. This is the result.

As certain as the sun goes down
Each evening in the west,
Enlightenment shall gain its ground
Wherever takes hold good sense.
For surely I am no mere tool
For use of all and sundry fool
To obey your mere commanding.

The winds of change, you try in fear,
To inhibit, but in vain.
For none shall choose to lend his ear
To your words of disdain.
You make decrees for all the nation
Subject to interpretation;
Thus, injustice is born.

Judges are made of men like that,
Who plainly cannot pronounce
Right from wrong better than a cat
When upon its prey does pounce.
The whip and flail the poor man feels,
No entreaties, no appeals.
Only well the rich will bribe

The poor man who finds little aid
His life's an arduous haul.
Should he but steal a loaf of bread
From a man who has it all
To gaol he's sent, once he is caught.
Disgrace shall ever be his lot,
Pardon never forthcoming.

Yet, if a man from higher strain
In case he gets his hands on
A fortune, he shall bear no shame
And then if should he call on
His kith and kin to make amends
The matter is brought to an end
Dismissed as indiscretion.

Who can help if fortune deemed
That one not be well bred?
The fruits of toil from such men gleaned
Are which the rich are fed.
Hence all honour is thus bestowed
On whom to it is greatly owed:
On he who always toils.

Reflections on the Universe[4]

The firmament yields its eastern bounds
Proclaiming the sun's approach.
As light lays claim to all the grounds
She beholds on her encroach.
She bids the world for her make way,
Her radiance imparting.
She reigns but till the end of day
Taking leave, westward departing.

The sands of time stand never still
Nor the sun in its celestial stride.
No worldly might, despite its will
Can shore up the temporal tide.
Nature holds ever to her plan
Assured her ways are sound.
She cares not for the woes of man;
She tramples them into the ground.

---

[4] **Authors note**: I once got to follow along with my father to Eskilstuna and travelled at a good time. When we got to Svista and Kvinnersta near Eskilstuna, I saw the sunrise. I thought of the splendid sight. This happened back in around 1892. Even though I was only 15 years old, I came upon the notion that I needed to describe the cosmos, which I wrote down once I got home. I have thought many times about how wonderful it is that such happens. I was born on 9 May 1877.

And what is man? If truth be told,
A mere being that walks the earth.
What nature will have us see, behold!
Until then, apt words are dearth.
I am but nothing, for I know not
The cosmos in detail
As darkness clouds all of my thoughts,
Faith must act, where mind will fail.

Upon the soil, the world of green,
There's increase, prolific and lush.
Among carnal beings too can be seen
Such a propagating rush.
But how did it all first come about?
My grasp of it does fail.
Despite my travails to find out
I toil to no avail.

I merely see a wondrous thing
Sprung from the great divine
The breath of life, I thus conclude,
Is of miraculous design.
Everything has a role to play.
Let us thus not wander
From our duties. Lest we should stray
And life's true value squander.

We say the earth moves through the sky,
But wherefrom comes such notion?
Indeed, we do not know just why.
Moreover, the earth is in motion
Around her axis, but where attached
Is harder to explain.
Something we all just know as fact
Is not so clear and plain.

Toward the heavens, fix your gaze,
Toward stars too many to number.
Behold! The moon commands its place,
Its light not to be encumbered.
By the ravages of time or storm at sea,
Its luminescence far too vast,
Far beyond the light we see
By the lonely candle cast.

Into dust our deeds shall fade
In the face of His creation.
Into our eternal bed we're laid,
A grave, our remuneration.
When at last it's time to rest
Some for us shall mourn.
Yet, we return to our most cherished nest:
The earth from whence we were born.

The evanescent memory

I could not turn my gaze awry,
When upon the grove I did espy
One lonely flower, so pure and fair.
Perhaps it can still be found there
              For me to behold.

Never shall I forget this time,
A moment deep within my mind.
Should my journey take me up the mound
Should my vessel run aground
              The memory persists.

Of all the treasures of the earth,
None I find surpasses your worth.
Yet to come forth and of you take hold
I just could not; I still recalled
              How courage failed me.

I hoped to bask in your delight
And forget my pain, forget my blight.
But soon I reach my journey's end,
Alas, not worthy my way to wend
            To see and have you.

Should my flower in the wind now bend,
The hand of God shall lift her again.
The master who foregoes all such things,
A hero greater than all kings,
            He ventured to live.

May I proclaim in words alone
My delight in calling you my own.
May we meet in our garden stead,
For time eternal, we two to spread
            Our radiant joy.

The Wayward Child

If only I knew just what path to take
Which would lead me on my way back home,
I would but persist, though my limbs so ache,
Exhausted with languor to the bone.
My mother and father, at home in tears,
They know not my fortune, ill or good.
Will they see again, in spite of their fears,
The child who once headed to the woods.

As I wandered from home one morning bright,
But for sweet berries was I yearning.
Now I find, just as many others might,
My thoughts are only of returning.
How my frail body now trembles with fear.
Think, if the forest harbours wild beasts!
The embrace of night envelops me near.
Lest I become an animal's feast!

Here beside the pine I shall take my rest.
Oh father, oh mother, come find me!
To rush back, I need receive no behest.
I turn aback, the forest behind me.
Here all alone, and feeling oh so cold,
But above in the heavens I see,

A little star shining brightly and bold.
How kindly she smiles down at me.

Indeed, I think the bright star in the skies
Is the lone child in the forest deep
But as soon as he shuts his two eyes
The child then enjoys a restful sleep
And finds himself drifting into a dream
Lost to his slumbering condition
Then face many a danger, so it seems
But which cannot come to fruition

Indeed, it was just as the child had feared,
That he was missed at the hearth and home.
And his mother's eyes were filled with tears
As his loved ones through the forest roamed.
To find the child who wandered astray,
The child who drifts on bewildering course.
And when he had found he had lost his way,
Perhaps then he shed tears of remorse.

And just as they searched, they suddenly stood
When a sobbing sound, seemed to be heard.
If indeed that was the sound deep in the wood,
'twas received as a foreboding word.
A few steps more and I hear someone say,
See! Look what we find under the pine!

The child we seek, and whom we shall take away
Back home in his father's arms consigned.

What joy they feel once they are home again
A pondering in their minds comes about
They all now see their affection remains;
The flame of love cannot be put out
Thus, the journey served as a good lesson,
And they took it to heart when they learned:
At times, misery becomes a blessing
Much was gained in the way events turned

Lest you e'er tell a child prone to wander
That the world to him only pose threat.
For he on such words will then ponder
And recall nothing more than such fret.
Instead, fill his mind with a world so kind
Where nothing but bliss and peace have their way
Naught of such fears shall he hold in his mind
If some time he should wander astray

What Love is Worth[5]

A loving maiden, kind and fair,
Of all things in creation,
Means more than any precious wares
And grants her love elation.
Seek not for treasures and worldly loot.
Ruin comes to those in such pursuit.

For he who worships but his purse
Is unworthy to hear
A wife, whose voice in song or verse
Would reach into his ear.
Verily, he shall never find
The true bliss that he left behind.

And he who keeps this thought in mind
Can find words to expound
The humble truth that lay behind
How true joy can be found.

---

[5] **Author's note:** I was inspired to write this poem when a boy in my neighbourhood became a farmhand in an adjacent parish. He greatly disliked the way the youth behaved when gathered together for some joyful purpose. The sons and daughters gathered into one group, while the farmhands and maids formed another!

Yet, fruitless it is such method to show.
If only they chose, all men would know.

Nothing found on land or at sea
Can stain the soul of man
As opulence and vanity.
On that, I firmly stand.
"Should you find that you want for naught,
Then until death be ne'er distraught."

Though may I please admonish you
Not to think I say
That there's no sense in wealth accrued,
But rather think this way:
Practical, all things are not.
'tis but one of many lessons taught.

I have heard many people say
That he who receives this
Becomes rich and thereby holds sway
Thus, he finds happiness.
What sacrilege! So low, so base!
I find no words for such a disgrace.

For such a home shall house no bliss.
That's obvious and clear.
Unless love and tenderness

Those found within cohere.
Such peace it brings, such joy in life,
Above all things, to love one's wife.

For many a man each day laments
The things that he has not.
Such bugbear in his mind cements
His soul with envy fraught.
What burden is such tendency.
No joy is had in jealousy.

I beg you now my counsel heed
And find a loyal match.
For whom you hold great love indeed,
Pray unto her attach.
Think fondly of the one you hold
More precious than a throne of gold.

For surely no one can ensure
That justice here shall reign.
Great wrongs arise and shall endure
In mammon's vast domain,
Yet only present in this life.
The grave shall offer no such strife.

There are many who are but blind
To the treasures that they bear.
As fortune smiles, you shall find,
On those who are aware.
Are not your sight, your feet, your hands
Worth more than all exotic lands?

Have you not much thought far beyond
Such simple craven greed?
If not, I fear your days be long
And arduous, indeed.
For avarice, it quickly breeds
Evil of which a proverb reads.

Why did I write the lines above?
Because, I hope to warn
That some of those who choose a love
'tween heart and coin are torn.
Heed my words and your heart follow.
Without love, pursuits are hollow.

The Cabin Boy[6]

At harbour, the ship rocked in the waves.
Its mast stood tall and proud.
The lanyards sung a song so brave
Defying the storm so loud.

Said the captain unto every man,
"Come, sailors, collect your due
And head for town, with pay in hand,
And delight in what pleases you."

The cabin boy joins in the horde
As they make their way on land.
To the tavern they head, all in accord,
As custom would demand.

Oh what delight the seamen take,
But the boy shyly refrains.
As ne'er he saw drink but make
For misery and pain.

---

[6] **Author's note:** I heard this life story at a temperance meeting many years ago. The speaker assured me that the events were true. At that time, I thought that the story was so good so I just had to write it down. Once I returned home, I wrote this poem as a memory.

"Have a glass, my boy, and you shall be
Merry, mirthful and jolly."
So says a sailor, full of glee,
Unaware of such folly.

"Never shall I be seen to swill",
Swore the boy, the men in a daze.
And then the horde tried every means
To make him change his ways.

At last, they asked the boy pray tell
Them why he chooses not
To partake in what they love so well,
The best thing to be sought.

The lad then begins to recall
A boyhood dark and grim,
A speech that lowered glasses all.
Not one drop crossed a brim.

"Bliss prevailed within our walls.
Happiness was our dear guest.
No pain of want did us befall.
Ne'er we lacked for life's best.

"Opulence possessed we not,
Yet there was love in our abode.
And forget the roses, I cannot
Which grew tall along the road.

"But the day came when fortune turned
Away from my home, my keep
And the set the stage for what I learned
Brings many a cause to weep.

"My father to the tavern went
And in not much time became
A loyal patron whose coin he spent,
A lush who ensnared remained.

"My mother by the window wept.
Her countenance showed languish.
Until at last my father stepped
Through the door – then came anguish.

"To the tavern all of his pay went.
Sufficed it not for what he craved.
Once all his coin at last was spent,
He pledged our home; he was a slave.

"One night, sat my mother again
awaiting her man, abashed.
She sat and stared, but all in vain.
By the drink, all dreams are dashed.

"When sunrise came, all hope was lost.
My father come home on a grate.
He drank so much his life it cost.
I pray you not share his fate.

"In torrents flowed my mother's tears.
Her young ones wailed in despair.
What of her dreams for future years?
Cursed be the drink's mortal snare.

"A sombre mood had struck us here.
I was, though young, eldest still.
It then occurred to mother dear
To protect us from the swill.

"She begged I give my solemn word
Which I now with you shall share
To renounce the gift that had interred
My father – this, I did swear.

"I took an oath on all things divine
Ne'er to taste that dreadful drink.
I recall I took her hand in mine.
Of that oath I gravely think.

"Make no mistake! I kept my word
I gave next to the body.
As bliss away from me was spurred.
What you call joy is shoddy."

Said now the sailor who wanted most
To see the lad have a swallow,
"Lest into that snare you shall coast.
Keep your promise, the straight path follow.

"Permit me find paper to write
A pledge solemnly composed.
Ne'er I return to drunken blight.
King Alcohol has been deposed."

He wrote a note; he signed his name
And best of all, before long,
The sailors who to the tavern came
Signed on, and the drink was foregone.

When then they returned to their ship,
The captain was lost for words.
How could they be, after such a trip,
Sober, with no ruckus heard?

The sailor who had led the herd
Came forth to explain the tale.
They took to heart the young boy's words
And broke free from gin and ale.

The captain asked to see the pledge
And he signed his name with ardour.
Now all the men aboard the ketch
Set sail to Temperance Harbour.

You've now heard how a heart so pure
Saved men from ruinous ploy.
The steadfast are but rarely lured.
May we learn from this young boy.

On Arrogance

I sighted at Lindholm one midsummer's day
A gentleman on ostentatious display.
He strutted and pranced through the palace estate.
No power on earth could his ego deflate.

His form and figure were so hard to see
For his person was cloaked in rife vanity.
My thoughts cannot rest; I just have to say,
How long will he live to be boastful this way?

What is it all worth to be shallow and vain?
Time turns all men frail, then they suffer in pain.
"Pride goeth before a fall", surely he's read.
I pray that he has such misfortune ahead.

Now, lest you need ask me how this man was dressed
He wore robes of grey, like so many possess.
I dare not guess where this man had his abode.
Perhaps by that river where pride overflowed.

Should ever he heed what my rhyme thus exhorts
I hope he will think about how he comports
And endeavour to change and not act the same.
Lest ever he walk in pride's ugly shame.

But understand well, all who lend me an ear.
Words can never say how I hold you so dear.
It is not for you that these harsh words are meant,
But to every man haughty and arrogant.

Various Thoughts
(Childhood Faith)

The things we've done in the past year,
No victory can compare.
While striving to our goal come near,
We did all that we could dare.
There is one thing to keep in mind.
Reflect on it and soon we'll find,
That each of us will have seen
That too lax in the struggle we've been.

Yes, faults and failings we possess.
Perfection's not of this world.
Still, there is much we can address
And learn how success unfurls.
For through the light we shine so bold
And through the spring that ne'er goes cold
That light will lead us to our goals.
The spring shall quench our thirsty souls.

Through union shall concord prevail
Fraternal with the same aim.
Ne'er shall ill words mark our travails
Or our steel will defame.
We'll focus tightly on the goal.
Under the yoke, we shall not fall.
Soon we receive our labour's fruit
Our right to such, none dare dispute.

If we from worldly things depart
And fix our gaze on high.
What shall we think? What words impart?
How do we dare reply?
Yes, often thoughts do us enthral.
We fantasise, expounding all.
If we explained so much we could,
Much would remain misunderstood

We think of how things ought not be
And how they should be instead.
Our trust in common sense put we,
But frustrating tears we shed.
Not all things have a reason why,
When clarity of thought runs dry.
All those who in this way seek God
Are doomed to fail, their method flawed.

For some secrets of life from man are masked.
Not all things is he meant to know.
The answer to every question asked,
"Where shall one flee, indeed where shall one go?"
Well, one need but use simple trick
And then a miracle is quick.
The kind of faith children possess
Is the source of worldly success.

Something About Spring

Nature awakes, at last, from her slumber
As the springtime sun sheds her pure light.
The hills and the valleys all echo with song
And welcome the season with delight.
All creatures on earth rejoice.
Life's a gem without compare.
Should you still face troubles,
In order put your affairs.

For nothing on earth does please a young man
As the approach of spring every year.
When many an image abounds in his mind
And hopes for the future appear.
Such thoughts rise to the heavens
Building castles in the air.
For elated joy fills his breast
When comes springtime so fair.

We often observe both maiden and youth
Finding a new friend when blossoming starts.
In the winter's cold grasp, they remained so reserved
But the warmth of the sun opens their hearts.
The lilies sway in the breeze
And bow in humility.
Making their place 'tween the lindens,
Though mere plants they may be.

How lovely in the summer it is but to wander
Hand-in-hand with a friend through a lush dale.
Then turn to proclaim one's affection so dearly
Under the chirping of birds, both sparrows and quails.
Nature herself is heard speaking
And whispers both hope and glee.
Elated we hear the birds singing
Way up from the top of a tree.

How brightly the flowers create a new Eden
Sumptuous and lush in the surge of the sun.
And splendid the sweet
flower seems out in the heath.
As far as we can see, worries have we none.
So may we all take much delight
In the fragrant flowers fair.
May our souls likewise find reprieve
From darkness and despair.

Nature is fickle, as many surely find.
It often plays a role of mere deceit.
When happiness looms, it oft disappears
Claiming innocence, but prone to cheat.
For roses all lose their colour.
Such has always been the way.
Therefore we should all remember
All things on earth pass away.

Quickly, the flowery season evanesces.
It rushes forward; nothing stands in its way.
When bloom falls all its beauty fades with it.
The cloak is unfolded and conceals the display.
But the true worth of all things remains
In the field, when harvest is nigh.
The reaper then collects the yield
And in the barn stores it high.

A harvest is coming, but we know not the time.
Its arrival, only the reaper knows.
We know only today that one more day has passed
Now one day fewer, before it no further goes.
In the abode made out of humus
To the seasons naught is prone.
He who keeps such abodes filled
Ascends to the highest of thrones.

A Sinner's Struggling Soul[7]

And now I take my pen in hand,
And faithfully convey
My struggle toward God's command
Before I found the way.
Though many errors I may write,
I feel bound to record
My journey that would set me right
With Jesus Christ my Lord.

Of early life, there's naught to tell
We all knew childhood
In innocence and bliss I dwelled
So much is understood.
But then began my struggle long.
I sought to answers find
Of the nature of the world beyond
And of God's grand design.

---

[7] **Author's note:** As we all know, the biggest issue for man is the question concerning eternity. Many times have I heard declarations on this matter, and this poem is a summary of it all.

Just like so many men before,
I sought my life to feed.
Mere vanity I found, not more,
From which I'm not yet freed.
And I who sought so much to find,
With joy, my life I squandered.
My battered soul does me remind
On death, I now ponder.

Many a time I would be caught
Inside a church to pray.
And those inside the Lord's house sought
God's love-light to portray.
But a voice from deep inside me
Told me to pay no heed.
My worldly thoughts misguide me,
My soul ne'er to be freed.

They begged that I my ways do mend
While time was on my side.
Heaven and earth some time could rend
I had no time to bide.
The time we walk upon the earth
For heaven, we prepare.
And contemplate our soul's rebirth
When Jesus takes us there.

My friends held me in high regard
So I downplayed such thoughts
And feigned an utter disregard.
My true heart I showed not.
And though I tried hard to conceal
My true heart on the matter,
My spirit begged me to reveal
A soul that was so shattered.

Yet, when I a grave danger faced,
I'd call upon the Lord.
And in His hands, my life I placed
In keeping with His word.
But as soon as the danger passed,
At my weakness, I felt shame.
In my mind, I felt aghast
To call upon His name.

And if adversity I found,
Anxiety I faced,
I made a pledge not to be bound
By sin's profound disgrace.
For all good men should keep in mind
That setback often shows
Other ways and means to find
The bliss a saved man knows.

Many a night saw me repose
So empty and so weak
Soon I found I should share my woes.
To friends, I could not speak.
As from my friends, my ways do part
My feelings they deride.
I dared not hope a man of God
Was found on earth alive.

Indeed, it was my task to find
What the heathen world's about.
By his nature he is inclined
For the easy way out.
They worship something that they find
Pays back in the beyond.
And after death will give mankind
All that for which he's longed.

Of all the comforts that I found
What I treasured most dear
Was to turn from antics that abound
At which most laugh and jeer.
Yet, still it always seemed to me
That many would suggest
That I was like a raft at sea
Without anchor to rest.

Complexity is nature's way.
Of God I have no doubt.
Our wondrous earth, I cannot say
How else she come about.
For I had a revelation.
My heart finds no relief.
Forsake all worldly temptation
And in Jesus, believe.

My heart tries to tell me to pray
And the gift of God embrace.
With the sin I carry today,
I never shall find grace.
I endeavour then to repent
And call upon the Lord.
Humble I kneel with my knees bent
To hear his tranquil word.

He told me right then to begin
And Christ was all we need.
He washes away all our sin.
Call on him and be freed.
My tears then ran down to my chin
What ecstasy that day!
The relief that's felt when freed from sin
Is more than words can say.

No, words alone cannot convey
The peace within my breast.
Pray Jesus take your sins away
And bring your soul to rest.
Have you a pious heart within,
Which many no doubt do,
Ask Jesus to forgive your sin.
Let heaven receive you.

With every fibre, every grain,
I thank God for his grace.
He freed me of my sin, my pain,
Transgressions and disgrace.
Forgive me, Lord, when I go stray
Upon the broken path.
Again, You'll wash my sins away
And spare me from Your wrath.

Temperance Song

In spite of stormy weather
And dim of evening light,
Once more we come together
For the sake of our fight.
May we delight in knowing
Our goal is within reach.
The movement's ever growing
Our message for to teach.

Concern for loved ones abounds
But takes us from our task.
So let us not get bogged down.
Persistence to the last!
There are others so many
Who tacitly stand by
Whose hearts would beat aplenty
To hear our battle cry

Though many feel dejected
By their own hand they failed
Our counsel they rejected
Our guiding hand bewailed
Poor fellows have no power
To resist their stubborn drives
The drink their lives devours
Their time on earth deprives

A loving mother to her son
Will in all wisdom say,
"Lest I should see you be undone
Keep far out of harm's way.

Though I can always guard you,
While in my house you dwell.
But mind yourself in all you do
Once you bid me farewell."

And then a few years did elapse
'fore he came home again.
Having so revelled in, perhaps,
The company of friends.
His earnings all soon found their way
To the tavern's landlord.
His youthful joy turned to dismay,
Heartsease into discord.

And in oh so many a place
And so many a time,
No matter where he turned his face
He heard the same old rhyme.
"You know not what you're missing
In just one drink partake.
In truth, there's no dismissing
The merriment it makes."

Many a father heard the cries
Of children wanting bread.
In vain, and thus their turned their eyes
To mother dear, instead.
In order to convince themselves
That father's at the inn,
When he came home, the timid ones
Hid all around therein.

Oh righteous men and ladies kind,
Who are in years not rife,
It still remains for you to find
The passion of your life.
For once old age seizes you,
Your reward shall you gain.
The more a passion pleases you,
The more it gives again.

Alas, you may be thinking
That I have done the same.
Yes, once took to drinking.
I'd fallen into shame.
So you should also realise
Oh that our cause is just,
And share conclusion likewise
As all with good sense must.

Heed my words all those who do
Not of the drink partake.
Thus spirits have not left you
In their ruinous wake.
Listen not to any friends,
No matter what they say-
You are your charge, in the end.
You must mind you own way.

Consider while you're reading
Whether my words ring true.
For changes are exceeding
That your passion will find you.
I pray my words compelling

My reasoning thought sound.
And as I am done telling,
I now put my pen down.

Song

A little child am I.
All sin I now defy.
For I've been saved by Jesus
Who by my heart is nigh.

That's why I love to sing
'bout Jesus, King of Kings.
I wait for His loving hands
To take me home with Him.

How could I ask for more?
Dear Jesus, I implore,
Wash away the stain of sin.
My grace with God restore.

I do not fear my fate.
His coming I await.
Leave in the hands of Jesus
All things, both small and great.

Though sin around abounds,
Never my soul it hounds.
Safely, I wait with Jesus
Until the trumpet sounds.

I was a sinner, true.
From Him I ne'er withdrew.
No, I just prayed to Jesus
His promise shall come through.

Despite my stain of sin,
Lord Jesus let me in.
I sing for I am grateful,
Redemption I did win.

When evil stares at me,
Wherever I may be,
I'll simply wait for Jesus
Until He comes for me.

Song (composed 17 July 1899)

And let us now with heartfelt praise
Give thanks to God above.
Both old and young, your voices raise
A song of sincere love.
Together we have gathered here,
As many times before,
His grace to seek, our souls endear,
On Jesus' restful shore.

Now, all of our human weakness,
We pray God take away.
He would have us in true meekness,
All His commands obey.
I gave My life for you to save.
Stand loyal next to Me.
And you shall overcome the grave
And live eternally.

With every fibre of your soul,
For all that's good, thank God.
Through pain and grief he does console
Despite our ways so flawed
Praise be to Him, who bore no sin,
Yet, gave His life for you.

As found the holy book within
That we be born anew.

Let us rejoice, let us delight.
In word and song, we praise.
That we are guarded by the might
Of Jesus all our days.
And if off the path we wander
Onto a sinful track,
Once Jesus then sees us yonder
His hand shall lead us back.

Words alone cannot explain
What bliss is felt within.
For those whose hearts from sin abstain
And let Jesus come in.
Yet many are not so certain
If they're right with the Lord.
But come my life's final curtain,
I know my just reward.

In strife stand firm, yet so humble.
Pray Jesus stand by you.
If you suffer, do not grumble.
Recall what He shall do.
He'll take away all pain and grief.
The gift He grants is grand.

Our troubled hearts shall find relief,
Once victory is at hand.

So by no means dare we ponder
Or contemplate in vain.
And forbid that we should wonder
How God rules his domain!
For not all answers are given.
Such was not meant to be.
So let's strive to be forgiven,
Our saviour for to see.

For not a man in truth can say
That free from sin is he.
For none who ever lived a day
Escaped iniquity.
But he who turns to Jesus Christ
Shall of his sins be cleaned.
For 'twas the Lord who paid the price
And all our souls redeemed.

Song

Come, Lord Jesus, and mercy show
Your children in their wayward life
And save Your people in times of woe
From sin and all bitter strife.

For our hearts are lifted yet again.
He comes and allays all our fright.
He relieves all sorrow and pain
And shares His radiance bright.

He shines with a light so clear, so true.
He sets us all on the right way.
In faith, we await His beckon to
Come home with Him, ever to stay.

I implore you all, who on earth still dwell,
In true faith, heed now what I say.
What becomes of your soul, you cannot tell,
When in time you must pass away.

Pray turn from your ways, while you still can
And lift your burdens from your chest.
Know that your faith in the Son of Man
Shall put your mind and soul at rest.

CONTENTS